W9-CFI-572

Storm
SURGE
The Science of **Hurricanes**

HEADLINE SCIENCE

by Don Nardo

Content Adviser:
Roberta M. Johnson, Ph.D., Director, Education and Outreach,
University Corporation for Atmospheric Research

Science Adviser:
Terrence E. Young Jr., M.Ed., M.L.S.,
Jefferson Parish (Louisiana) Public School System

Reading Adviser:
Rosemary G. Palmer, Ph.D., Department of Literacy,
College of Education, Boise State University

Compass Point Books • 1710 Roe Crest Drive • North Mankato, Minnesota 56003

Library of Congress Cataloging-in-Publication Data
Nardo, Don, 1947–
  Storm surge : the science of hurricanes / by Don Nardo.
     p. cm. — (Headline science)
  Includes bibliographical references and index.
  ISBN 978-0-7565-4055-5 (library binding)
1. Hurricanes—Juvenile literature. 2. Storm surges—Juvenile literature.
I. Title. II. Series.
  QC944.2.N37 2009
  551.55'2—dc22   2008037573

Editor: Jennifer VanVoorst
Designers: Ellen Schofield and Ashlee Suker
Page Production: Ashlee Suker
Photo Researcher: Svetlana Zhurkin
Illustrator: Cory Johnson, XNR Productions, Inc.

Art Director: LuAnn Ascheman-Adams
Creative Director: Joe Ewest
Editorial Director: Nick Healy
Managing Editor: Catherine Neitge

Photographs ©: NOAA/NESDIS, cover (bottom); NASA, cover (inset, left), 16, 20; NOAA/National Weather Service
Collection, cover (inset, middle), 11, 26, 27, 34; Bob Randall/iStockphoto, cover (inset, right), 5; Rodrigo Arangua/
AFP/Getty Images, 7; Gary Williams/Getty Images, 9; Jerry Grayson/Helifilms Australia PTY Ltd./Getty Images,
10; Express Newspapers/Getty Images, 12; AP Photo/*The Chronicle*, James Nielsen, 14; NOAA/Flying With NOAA
Collection, 17, 24; Joe Raedle/Getty Images, 22, 35; AP Photo/Wilfredo Lee, 25; AP Photo/Andy Newman, 28;
Jay Directo/AFP/Getty Images, 30; rest/iStockphoto, 31; Kimberly Deprey/iStockphoto, 32; Mario Tama/Getty
Images, 37; Lisa F. Young/iStockphoto, 39; Pat Semansky/Getty Images, 40; mostlymozart/iStockphoto, 41; Mat-
thew Hinton/AFP/Getty Images, 42; Robyn Beck/AFP/Getty Images, 43.

Visit Compass Point Books on the Internet at *www.compasspointbooks.com*
or e-mail your request to *custserv@compasspointbooks.com*

HURRICANE KATRINA DEVASTATES U.S. GULF STATES

>>> Damian Carrington
New Scientist
August 30, 2005

Hurricane Katrina smashed into the Gulf coast of the U.S. on Monday, causing at least 50 deaths and widespread destruction. The storm had weakened a little before hitting land early on Monday, going from the maximum Category 5 down to 4. But sustained wind speeds of up to 150 miles (240 kilometers) per hour and a coastal storm surge of up to 6.7 meters (22 feet) above normal tide levels led to severe damage across Louisiana, Mississippi and Alabama. The peak storm surge was 8.5 m (28 ft), according to the U.S. National Hurricane Center (NHC). Mississippi governor Haley Barbour said: "It came in on Mississippi like a ton of bricks. It is a terrible storm." He said his worst fear is "that there are a lot of dead people."

Governor Haley Barbour's fears about Hurricane Katrina's death toll were not misplaced. At least 1,836 people died in the disaster. It also caused more than $81 billion in property damages. In addition, tens of thousands of people in Louisiana and Mississippi became homeless. These and other factors made Katrina one of the most devastating hurricanes ever to strike the United States.

Clearly, Katrina was an unusually strong hurricane that did a lot of damage. But *all* hurricanes are potentially dangerous to property and life. This is because a hurricane is one of the largest and most powerful weather events in nature. A hurricane is a giant storm that forms in the open ocean. Such storms can range from fewer than

A tree, uprooted by Hurricane Katrina's strong winds, fell against a car and house in New Orleans' Ninth Ward.

News changes every minute, and readers need access to the latest information to keep current. Here are a few key search terms to help you locate up-to-the-minute hurricane headlines:

Atlantic hurricane season

hurricane hunters

hurricane warning

hurricane watch

National Hurricane Center

National Oceanic and Atmospheric Administration

Pacific hurricane season

Saffir-Simpson scale

100 miles (160 kilometers) across to as many as 600 miles (960 km) across. To qualify for hurricane status, a storm must generate winds of 74 miles (118 km) per hour or higher.

NAMING THE MONSTERS

Hurricane is not the only name given to these monster storms. That is what they are called when they form in the Atlantic Ocean, Gulf of Mexico, and eastern Pacific Ocean. But when they appear in the western Pacific

region, including Japan, they are called typhoons. In the Indian Ocean, Bay of Bengal, and Australia, people call them cyclones.

Hurricanes also receive individual, personalized names. Meteorologists, scientists who study weather phenomena, formally began this practice in 1953. That year, the U.S. National Hurricane Center in Miami, Florida, started assigning each new hurricane a woman's name in alphabetical order. Among the first were Barbara,

Carol, and Dolly in 1953. In 1979, the female names began to alternate with male names. Some famous giant storms with male names have been Allen in 1980, Keith in 2000, and Gafilo in 2004. Today these names are assigned each year by the World Meteorological Organization, an agency of the United Nations.

Hurricane Keith, the strongest hurricane of the 2000 Atlantic hurricane season, damaged great swaths of Central America.

DAMAGE FROM WIND AND WATER

Whatever one chooses to call them—hurricanes, typhoons, or cyclones—these storms have the potential to do enormous damage. Destruction often results from the high winds a hurricane generates. For example, Hurricane Carol unleashed winds of up to 115 mph (184 kph). Obviously, the stronger the wind speeds are, the more potential there is for damage.

To help anticipate possible damage, meteorologists use a special scale. It classifies or grades hurricane wind forces. Called the Saffir-Simpson scale, it is named for the two scientists who devised it in 1971—Herbert Saffir and Bob Simpson. The scale has five numbered levels, called categories. The first and lowest—a Category 1 storm—produces winds from 74 to 95 mph (120 to 152 kph). It generally produces some minimal damage to trees and mobile homes. A Category 2 hurricane, with winds from 96 to 110 mph (154 to 176 kph), causes major damage to mobile homes and minimal damage to standard homes. In Category 3, winds range from 111 to 130 mph (178 to 208 kph). Some trees are uprooted, and small buildings sustain moderate damage. Then comes Category 4, with punishing winds of 131 to 155 mph (210 to 248 kph). Such a storm does significant

damage to homes and other small structures and destroys many trees. Most damaging of all is a Category 5 storm, with winds greater than 155 mph (248 kph). It can produce extensive, even catastrophic, damage to buildings, forests, and beaches.

Strong winds are not the only aspect of hurricanes that can cause destruction of property and loss of life. Serious flooding also often occurs when a hurricane strikes. Some of the flooding results from heavy rains that fall from the storm's swirling cloud masses.

Other flooding can come from the powerful storm surge a hurricane can

SAFFIR-SIMPSON HURRICANE SCALE

Category	Wind Speed	Storm Surge	Notable Hurricanes (category at landfall)
Category 1	74–95 mph (120–152 kph)	4–5 feet (1.2–1.5 m)	Hurricane Lili, 2002
Category 2	96–110 mph (154–176 kph)	6–8 feet (1.8–2.4 m)	Hurricane Ivan, 2008
Category 3	111–130 mph (178–208 kph)	9–12 feet (2.7–3.6 m)	Hurricane Katrina, 2005
Category 4	131–155 mph (210–248 kph)	13–18 feet (3.9–5.4 m)	Hurricane Charley, 2004
Category 5	>155 mph (>248 kph)	>18 feet (>5.4 m)	Hurricane Andrew, 1992

Sources: National Hurricane Center

Hurricanes of any category can do real damage to the natural and man-made worlds, whether through wind or water.

generate. A storm surge is a wall of water. As a hurricane moves across the ocean, its spiraling winds push water outward, creating a moving mound of liquid. Low air pressure at the center of the storm also causes the water to rise. When the rising water approaches a coastline, the water piles up even higher. In 2005, Hurricane Katrina, a Category 3 storm, produced a storm surge more than 20 feet (6 meters) high. The unusually high storm surge caused some of the levees surrounding New Orleans to fail. The

NOW YOU KNOW

Only three hurricanes have ever made landfall in the United States as Category 5 storms—an unnamed storm that struck the Florida Keys in 1935, Hurricane Camille, which hit Mississippi in 1969, and Hurricane Andrew, which plowed into southeastern Florida in 1992.

New Orleans is mostly below sea level. The failure of its levees allowed water from the storm surge to penetrate the city, which held the water like a bowl.

city was badly flooded, and thousands of homes were destroyed.

SOME MEMORABLE HURRICANES

In fact, Katrina did more property damage than any of the hundreds of hurricanes that have struck the United States since its founding. But several past hurricanes have been memorable for other reasons. Some have even shaped the course of history. For example, in 1565, a hurricane scattered a fleet of French war ships and allowed the Spanish to capture a French fort in what is now Florida. In 1609, a fleet of ships carrying settlers from England to Virginia was struck by a hurricane. Some of the ships were damaged, and part of the fleet was grounded on Bermuda, a group of islands in the Atlantic. These passengers became the first people to live on Bermuda.

Similarly, the so-called Great Hurricane of 1780 struck a number of Caribbean islands. The Revolutionary War, in which the Americans fought for independence from Great Britain, was then under way. The storm helped the Americans by destroying a number of British ships docked in the Caribbean.

Some more recent hurricanes made the record books because of their high wind speeds. In 1992, for instance, Hurricane Andrew generated winds up to 165 mph (264 kph). The 1935 Labor Day Hurricane struck the Florida Keys with winds reaching 200 mph (320 kph). And Typhoon Nancy, which hit Japan in 1961, produced astonishing 215-mph (344-kph) winds.

Other giant storms have been infamous for the terrible death tolls they caused. The worst example in the United States was the hurricane

In 1992, Hurricane Andrew's Category 5 winds drove a piece of plywood through the trunk of a palm tree.

that destroyed Galveston, Texas, in 1900. Estimates for the number of people killed ranged from 8,000 to 12,000. Even worse was the disaster caused in 1975 by Typhoon Nina, which smashed into China. Several large dams collapsed, and more than 100,000 people died.

The largest loss of life attributed to such a storm occurred in 1970. The Bhola Cyclone devastated East Pakistan (now Bangladesh), drowning at least 500,000 people. These horrific figures show the great destructive power of large hurricanes. They also provide ample motivation to better understand how these storms form and how to prepare for them. ◤

After the devastating 1970 hurricane, children on the island of Bhola waded through floodwater looking for friends, family, and dry land.

TROPICAL STORM DEAN COULD BECOME ATLANTIC HURRICANE

Reuters
August 14, 2007

Tropical Storm Dean formed in the Atlantic Ocean midway between Africa and the Caribbean on Tuesday and could become the first Atlantic hurricane of the 2007 season later in the week, U.S. forecasters said. At 5 p.m. EDT, the center of Dean was located about 1,390 miles east of the Lesser Antilles [Islands] and was charging west at about 21 miles per hour (34 kph), the hurricane center said. Dean's top sustained winds were about 40 mph (64 kph). It was expected to gradually strengthen and become a hurricane. ... The storm could be a Category 3 hurricane with winds of up to 127 mph (204 kph) in five days, forecasters said.

Tropical Storm Dean did indeed go on to become a major hurricane. It surpassed the forecasted Category 3 status and became a Category 5 hurricane. Packing winds up to 165 mph (264 kph), it slammed into eastern Mexico. More than 40 people died, and property damages were in the billions of dollars.

NATURE'S GIANT HEAT ENGINES

How did the tropical storm named Dean form and then grow into a hurricane? In essence, Dean and other hurricanes are giant heat engines, the largest produced by nature. An average hurricane contains heat energy equivalent to 200 times the total electrical power generated by human civilization.

All that warmth comes from Earth's oceans, which contain large stores of heat energy. Not surprisingly, the biggest concentrations of heat exist in the warm waters lying just north and south of the equator. Small amounts of heat in such waters can produce small thunderstorms. And larger amounts of heat can produce large thunderstorms and even hurricanes.

People braved the winds and rain of Hurricane Dean as it made landfall near Martinez de la Torre, Mexico, in August 2007.

HEADLINE SCIENCE

In order for a hurricane to form, the water temperature must be between 80 and 81 degrees Fahrenheit (27 degrees Celsius) down to a depth of about 150 feet (46 m).

When an area of ocean meets these conditions, some of the heat rises. This produces a mild updraft of water vapor. The rising water vapor soon encounters cooler air located a few thousand feet above the ocean. The meeting of warm and cool air causes much of the water vapor to condense into water droplets, which form bands of clouds. Heat is released in the process.

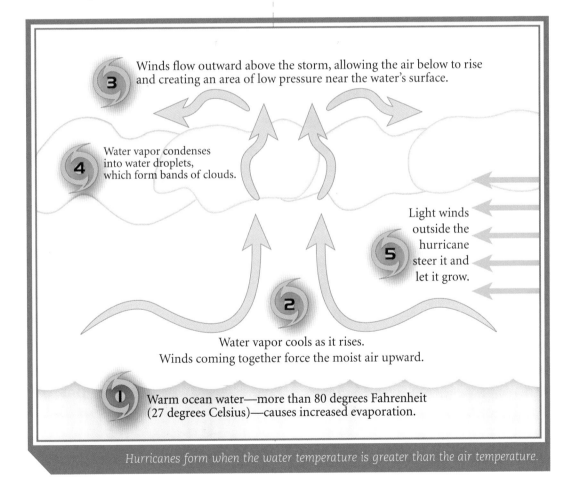

3 Winds flow outward above the storm, allowing the air below to rise and creating an area of low pressure near the water's surface.

4 Water vapor condenses into water droplets, which form bands of clouds.

5 Light winds outside the hurricane steer it and let it grow.

2 Water vapor cools as it rises. Winds coming together force the moist air upward.

1 Warm ocean water—more than 80 degrees Fahrenheit (27 degrees Celsius)—causes increased evaporation.

Hurricanes form when the water temperature is greater than the air temperature.

The rising warm air also creates an area of low air pressure near the water's surface. Then a sort of chain reaction can occur. The lower the pressure gets, the more warmth rises from the ocean. This causes the air pressure to drop even further. As the cycle repeats itself, more and more heat is generated, and the storm gains strength.

If the winds produced in such a thunderstorm reach 21 mph (34 kph), experts call it a tropical depression. If the wind speed increases to exceed 35 mph (56 kph), the tropical depression becomes a tropical storm. It remains so until the winds reach 74 mph (118 kph), at which point the storm officially becomes a hurricane.

STRUCTURAL FEATURES

Having developed into a hurricane, the storm displays certain characteristic structural features. One of the more prominent ones is the eye. It is located at the center of the storm, where the winds and clouds rotate around it. The eyes of hurricanes usually measure

The crew of the space shuttle Atlantis *photographed the eye of* Typhoon Saomai *as it swirled in the Pacific Ocean near Taiwan.*

from about 12 to 50 miles (19 to 80 km) across. In that zone, conditions are generally calm, with little or no wind or rain.

In contrast, the storm's strongest winds and rain exist along the outer edge of the eye. There, a circular, vertical wall of fierce, wind-driven clouds rises into the sky. Fittingly, experts call it the eye wall. Winds in the eye wall of 1968's Hurricane Camille reached an impressive 200 mph (320 kph).

Radiating outward from the eye wall are the hurricane's vast spiral bands (or spiral rain bands) of clouds. They swirl around the eye in a counterclockwise direction in the Northern Hemisphere—the region lying above the equator. In the Southern Hemisphere—below the equator—the bands move clockwise.

In fact, the spiral bands almost

The eye wall of Hurricane Katrina was photographed in August 2005 just south of its landfall in Louisiana.

always form within the regions lying between 5 and 15 degrees north or south of the equator. Only rarely do these giant storms originate fewer than 5 degrees from the equator. Cyclone Agni, which formed in the Indian Ocean in 2004, was one of the few exceptions.

It is important to note that a hurricane's spiral bands are not a solid mass of clouds. According to the University of Illinois Department of Atmospheric Sciences:

There are sometimes gaps in between these bands where no rain is found. In fact, if one were to travel between the outer edge of the hurricane to its center, one would normally progress from light rain to dry, back to slightly more intense rain again over and over, with each period of rainfall being more intense and lasting longer until reaching the eye. Upon exiting the eye and moving towards the edge of the hurricane, one would see the same events as they did going in, but in opposite order.

NOW YOU KNOW

When two hurricanes approach each other, the Fujiwara Effect (named for Japanese scientist Sakuhei Fujiwara) occurs. The storms revolve around a common center between them. If one is larger than the other, the smaller storm will orbit the bigger one.

HURRICANES ON THE MOVE

Most hurricanes develop during "hurricane season." This varies from one part of the world to another. In the Atlantic region, it runs from June 1 to November 30. Hurricane season in the eastern Pacific region lasts longer—from May 15 to November 30. And in Australia, most hurricanes form between early January and late March.

Whenever or wherever it forms, a hurricane remains almost always on

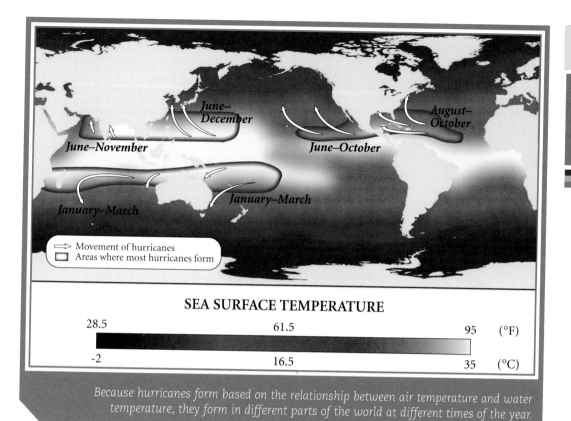

June–December

August–October

June–November

June–October

January–March

January–March

⇨ Movement of hurricanes
☐ Areas where most hurricanes form

SEA SURFACE TEMPERATURE

28.5	61.5	95	(°F)
-2	16.5	35	(°C)

Because hurricanes form based on the relationship between air temperature and water temperature, they form in different parts of the world at different times of the year.

the move. Over open ocean, it maintains an average speed of 10 to 20 mph (16 to 32 kph). As long as the waters the hurricane passes over are warm, the storm will maintain its strength or grow stronger.

In contrast, sometimes a moving hurricane encounters a patch of ocean with cooler water. In that case, the storm usually weakens. Its winds might even drop below 74 mph (120 kph), reducing it to tropical-storm status. In that case, one of two things will happen. Either the storm will continue to weaken, or it will regain its strength and become a hurricane again. For example, Agni went from tropical storm to cyclone and back to tropical storm. Then it intensified into a cyclone again before finally

Astronauts on board the space shuttle Columbia photographed a cyclone forming over the Tasman Sea between Australia and New Zealand.

weakening and dying.

The death of a hurricane can occur either over open ocean, as the storm moves over colder water, or over land. It usually happens considerably faster over land. When such a storm makes landfall, it no longer has warm water from which to draw strength. The great heat engine begins to shut down and quickly weakens into a big thunderstorm. It might still dump a lot of rain on inland regions, but its damaging winds rapidly disperse. The people living along the coast are safe, at least until another hurricane springs to life and threatens the area.

HOW STRONG IS THAT HURRICANE? JUST LISTEN

Science Daily
April 10, 2008

Knowing how powerful a hurricane is, before it hits land, can help to save lives or to avoid the enormous costs of an unnecessary evacuation. So far, there's only one surefire way of measuring the strength of a hurricane: Sending airplanes to fly right through the most intense winds and into the eye of the storm, carrying out wind-speed measurements as they go. Some MIT researchers think there may be a better, cheaper way of getting that crucial information. By placing hydrophones (underwater microphones) deep below the surface in the path of an oncoming hurricane, it's possible to measure wind power as a function of the intensity of the sound. The roiling action of the wind ... causes a rushing sound whose volume is a direct indicator of the storm's destructive power.

Before the modern age, people had no way of knowing if a hurricane was forming out in the ocean. On occasion, a ship might encounter the storm at sea. But chances were slim the vessel could make it back to land in time to give a warning. In fact, many of these ships were damaged or sunk by the high winds and large waves generated by hurricanes. Thus, for a long time most of these giant storms caught populated areas by surprise. Often many lives were lost and much property was damaged or destroyed.

This situation fortunately changed with the advent of modern scientific devices and methods. These include:

- airplanes that gather information by flying directly into hurricanes;
- radar devices that track storm movements;
- satellites that take pictures of

Meteorologists at the National Hurricane Center in Miami, Florida, monitor and analyze tropical weather patterns using a variety of high-tech tools.

hurricanes from high above;

- computers that predict how these storms will move.

Thanks to these and other methods, hurricanes can now be detected and tracked with much greater precision. As a result, these storms kill far fewer people than in the past.

RIDING THE WINDS

The first modern inventions that helped to forecast the formation and tracking of hurricanes were the telegraph and radio. Both appeared in the late 1800s and were perfected in the early 1900s. They allowed people to rapidly send information about oncoming storms to distant cities. Particularly helpful were ships equipped with radios. Weather observers at sea were now able to relay their observations about hurricanes and other weather conditions to land-based weather stations in mere seconds.

An even more valuable technology began to be used in 1944, near the end of World War II. It consists of airplanes flying directly into hurri-

canes to gather data. The adventurous individuals who perform this duty are often called hurricane hunters.

Today most of the American hurricane hunters operate out of two bases. One is the U.S. Air Force Reserve facility in Biloxi, Mississippi. It mainly uses a four-engine propeller craft—the WC-130J. The other base, in Tampa, Florida, is run by the National Oceanic and Atmospheric Administration (NOAA). The NOAA hurricane hunters use another four-engine prop plane—the WP-3D. These planes most

HEADLINE SCIENCE

NOW YOU KNOW

In 2005, Hurricane Katrina severely damaged the base used by hurricane hunters in Biloxi, Mississippi. Undaunted, they moved their operations to a base near Atlanta, Georgia, and kept flying. The Biloxi base has since been repaired and is back in operation.

Hurricane hunters fly planes directly into the eyes of hurricanes in order to collect data that will help scientists on the ground predict the storms' movements and intensity.

often carry a crew of six. It consists of a pilot, co-pilot, navigator, flight engineer, weather officer, and data-gathering expert.

A typical hurricane-hunting mission lasts about 10 or 11 hours. Some of this time is spent inside the hurricane's upper cloud bands. As one NOAA team member puts it, the plane slices "through the eye wall … buffeted by howling winds, blinding

NOW YOU KNOW

A remotely piloted (remote-controlled) aircraft—the *Aerosonde*—successfully flew into Tropical Storm Ophelia in 2005 and gathered data.

rain, hail, and violent updrafts and downdrafts before entering the relative calm of the storm's eye." During the turbulent flight, onboard instruments check wind speeds and take other measurements.

The crew also drops small devices, called GPS (Global Positioning System) dropsondes. Attached to parachutes, they plummet down into the storm.

They collect readings of temperature, humidity, air pressure, and wind speed, and send the data by radio waves to receivers in the plane.

ADVANCED OBSERVATION METHODS

Three other technologies that have

An Air Force technical sergeant loads a GPS dropsonde—a cardboard tube stuffed with sensors—into a launcher; as it falls, the dropsonde will collect and transmit important data about the storm.

improved detection and study of hurricanes are radar, satellites, and computers. The first of these advanced observation methods, radar, works on the principle of reflection. A transmitter sends out a burst of radio waves that strike a fixed or moving target. In this case, the target consists of a hurricane's cloud bands. The radio waves reflect off the water vapor in clouds and bounce back to a receiver. In this manner, weather observers can tell where the storm is and how fast it is moving. The National Weather Service began using radar this way in 1957. Today most weather stations employ a more advanced form of radar— Doppler radar—for this purpose.

As a hurricane-detecting tool, radar is most effective when a storm is approaching a coastline or already over land. The most reliable devices for spotting the formation of tropical storms and hurricanes in the open ocean are satellites. The first successful weather satellite was *TIROS* 1. It was launched by the United States in

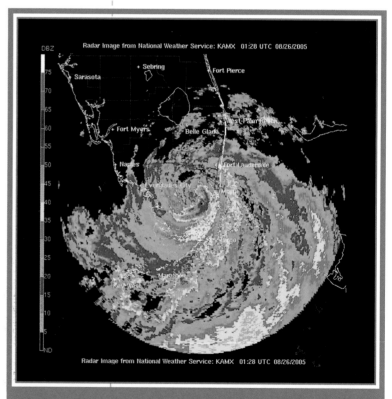

A 2005 radar image showed the eye of Hurricane Katrina as it passed just south of Miami, Florida.

1960. Today more advanced satellites routinely capture photos of ocean storms of all types and transmit them to ground-based weather stations. This allows forecasters to know exactly when and where a hurricane forms.

The amount of hurricane-related data collected each year by satellites, radar, aircraft, GPS dropsondes, and other sources is huge. It is too much for one or even several people to sort through, organize, and compare effectively. Computers do much of this work today. That allows weather experts more time to evaluate the results. Computers also use the data to make models of hurricane behavior. These suggest the most

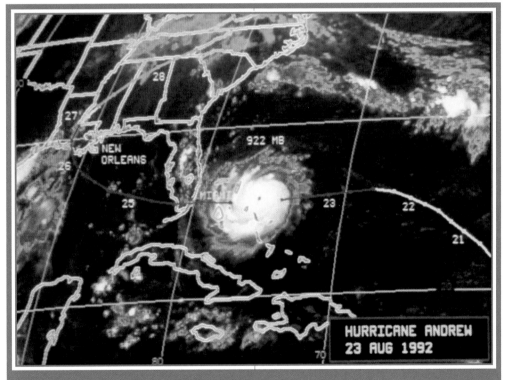

Infrared is another technology that scientists use to track hurricanes; it detects the heat that hurricanes give off and can be used to create detailed pictures of hurricanes and their movements.

National Hurricane Center Director Bill Read updated television viewers on the progress of Hurricane Gustav in August 2008.

likely paths a storm will take during a given time period.

PLENTY OF ADVANCE WARNING

In these ways, modern technology has revolutionized the study of hurricanes. It is now possible to track these storms with reasonable accuracy. It is still difficult to predict how intense the winds will become within a specific hurricane. But at least people who live on vulnerable coastlines can be confident of plenty of advance warning.

As a large storm approaches, local authorities first issue a hurricane watch. This report states that the hurricane poses a possible threat and might strike within 36 hours. If that threat becomes more imminent, the authorities issue a hurricane warning. It tells local residents that hurricane-force winds will likely affect their area in 24 hours or less. It is then up to these residents to make the necessary preparations to survive the storm's onslaught.

HURRICANES GETTING STRONGER, STUDY SUGGESTS

Sarah Graham
Scientific American
September 16, 2005

The devastation wreaked along the Gulf Coast by Hurricane Katrina has raised difficult questions about our ability to predict and prepare for natural disasters. The results of a new study suggest that there may be more Katrinas in the future. According to an analysis published today in *Science*, the number of Category 4 and Category 5 hurricanes has almost doubled in the past 35 years. ... Because tropical storms draw energy from ocean water to gain strength, it has been hypothesized that global warming—and the warmer waters associated with it—could lead to stronger hurricanes.

In recent years, a number of scientists have said the overall intensity of hurricanes seems to be increasing. These informal observations prompted a major study of hurricanes. Team members included Peter Webster, who teaches at the Georgia Institute of Technology; Judith Curry and Hai-Ru Chang, also of Georgia Tech; and Greg Holland, of the National Center for Atmospheric Research in Boulder, Colorado. These noted researchers looked at the number, duration, and intensity of all the hurricanes recorded around the globe from 1970 to 2004.

The team published the results of the controversial study in 2005. "What we found was rather astonishing," Webster stated. "In the 1970s, there was an average of about 10 Category 4 and 5 hurricanes per year globally. Since 1990, the number of Category 4 and 5 hurricanes has almost doubled, averaging 18 per year globally."

Curry stated it a different way. In the 1970s, she said, about 20 percent of hurricanes had Category 4 or 5

A woman and child braved the rain and floodwaters of Typhoon Sinlaku in Manila, Philippines, in September 2008.

status. But in the period from 1997 to 2007, roughly 35 percent of these storms were Category 4 or 5.

It is important to note that the researchers did not find any major increase in the *number* of large storms overall. On average, they found, about 87 to 90 hurricanes formed each year worldwide. The only exception was in the North Atlantic. The frequency of hurricanes increased there from about five to eight per year after 1995, the research showed.

GLOBAL WARMING THE CULPRIT?

Based on the study's results, Webster, his colleagues, and other scientists faced a burning question. Namely, what could be causing the recent increase in the number of strong hurricanes? Some researchers suggested that the culprit might be global warming. This consists of perceived increases in the temperature of our planet's atmosphere. Scientists have observed that such increases are melting glaciers and the North Pole's

ice cap at alarming rates. They also seem to be causing strange changes in global weather patterns. Some regions are regularly experiencing warmer-

Melting glaciers are a sign of global warming, a phenomenon that some scientists think could be affecting the intensity of hurricanes.

than-average summers. Other areas have been burdened by colder-than-average winters.

The vast majority of scientists now accept that global warming is a real phenomenon. Most think that human activity is the main cause. They say that the release of carbon dioxide and other gases by cars and factories is making the atmosphere warmer.

However, scientific opinions about global warming's connection to hur-

NOW YOU KNOW

According to scientists, the overall temperature of Earth's atmosphere rose at least half a degree between 1982 and 2007.

ricane intensity are decidedly mixed. On the one hand, a study published in 2007 supported the idea that global

Most scientists believe that carbon dioxide released into the atmosphere by factories, cars, and other human activity is contributing to global warming.

warming is responsible. A report by the U.S. Intergovernmental Panel on Climate Change stated that it is "more likely than not" that human-influenced climate change is making hurricanes stronger. "It is likely," the report said, "that future [hurricanes] will become more intense, with larger peak wind speeds and more heavy precipitation [rainfall]."

This theory suggests that the warming atmosphere is making the surface waters of parts of the oceans warmer. The increased heat stored in the water then becomes added fuel for hurricanes. When a hurricane passes over one of these warmer areas, it sucks up the heat. The storm becomes stronger than it would under normal conditions.

A NATURAL CYCLE?

On the other hand, a number of scientists say the link between global warming and hurricane strength is far from proved. Among them is Peter Webster, co-author of the 2005 Georgia Tech study. "We need a longer data record of hurricane statistics," he states. "And we need to understand more about the role hurricanes play in regulating the heat balance and circulation in the atmosphere and oceans."

In particular, Webster says, it is difficult to relate global warming to hurricane frequency. Why, he and other experts ask, does the overall number of hurricanes remain the same each year in most areas? If global warming is making the oceans warmer, it should be easier for hurricanes to form. So why is the overall annual number of hurricanes not rising? Also, why is the only rise in hurricane frequency observed in the North Atlantic?

One alternative theory is that both the number and intensity of hurricanes may vary naturally over time. In other words, these factors may be cyclic and normal, at least in the Atlantic Ocean. The cycle is called the Atlantic Multidecadel Oscillation. It seems to occur every 40 to 60 years.

Supporters of this theory point out that Atlantic hurricanes were fairly infrequent between 1900 and 1925. In contrast, from 1926 to 1960 they were decidedly more frequent than normal. In 1933, for instance, 21 Atlantic hurricanes formed. (That remained the record until 1995, when 28 hurricanes formed in the Atlantic.) Then, between 1960 and 1995, fewer hurricanes than normal formed in the Atlantic, followed by another rise after 1995.

It remains unclear why this cycle occurs, but most scientists think a definite pattern exists. However, if the cycle is indeed real, it does not rule out the contribution of global warming. Some researchers think that both the Atlantic Multi-decadel Oscillation and global warming may be affecting the intensity of hurricanes.

Hurricane Carol caused flooding along the North Atlantic Coast in 1954, during a more than 30-year period of increased hurricane activity.

UNRELIABLE DATA?

According to some experts, there is also a possibility that the Georgia Tech data is flawed. One is Chris Landsea, a meteorologist at NOAA's National Hurricane Center

Meteorologist Chris Landsea tracked the movement of Hurricane Dean, then a Category 4 storm, as it passed through the Caribbean in August 2007.

in Miami. He questions the increase in hurricane strength calculated by Webster's team. Landsea points out that the Georgia Tech data relies heavily on information gathered by satellites. But satellite technology was not nearly as good in the 1970s and 1980s as it is today. So the measurements of hurricanes taken in those decades are less accurate. That might mean that Webster's and his colleagues' conclusions are wrong.

These disagreements show that the question of hurricanes getting stronger has not been answered to everyone's satisfaction. Also, the jury is still out, so to speak, on whether global warming is involved. Clearly these issues require more study and more scientific debate. As scientists work to resolve these questions, we have the chance to witness the scientific process in action.

NEW ORLEANS SETS PLAN FOR HURRICANE EVACUATION

Adam Nossiter
The New York Times
August 29, 2008

With the storm Gustav newly elevated to hurricane status as it passes through the Caribbean and aims at the Gulf Coast, Mayor C. Ray Nagin said on Friday that a mandatory evacuation order was possible for Sunday. At that point, residents would be told, though not physically forced, to leave New Orleans, either in their own vehicles or on city-chartered buses and trains. On Saturday, officials here will start helping citizens without cars leave for shelters in northern Louisiana in gyms, churches and civic centers. Officials here estimate that as many as 30,000 of the poor, the elderly and the infirm might need help evacuating.

Whether or not hurricanes are getting stronger, the fact remains that even a weak hurricane poses real dangers to those living in coastal regions. In order to protect citizens, public officials in New Orleans and many other cities and towns along the U.S. Gulf Coast have implemented hurricane emer-gency plans. These plans, which can call for mandatory evacuation in certain circumstances, were largely prompted by the unusually active 2005 hurricane season. That year, the Atlantic produced 28 named tropical storms, 15 of which grew into hurricanes. Four of these became

New Orleans residents waited for buses and trains to evacuate them from the city as Hurricane Gustav approached the Gulf Coast in August 2008.

Category 5. In addition, four strong hurricanes struck U.S. coastlines.

In the aftermath of the devastating Hurricane Katrina, federal and state officials felt that it was better to be safe than sorry. Creating a wide-ranging hurricane preparation plan became a priority. States developed plans to address issues that would arise before, during, and after the crisis, including evacuation, traffic management, shelter, medical resources, communications, pet concerns, security, and donations. They organized drills to help public officials test the emergency systems and allow citizens to practice their own preparation plans.

A key aspect of hurricane emergency plans has to do with getting information to the public. This is because many local citizens have only sketchy ideas about how to prepare for large-scale hurricanes. These plans offer advice on how homeowners and other individual citizens can prepare. So do advisories from the American Red Cross and the Federal Emergency

Management Agency (FEMA). Most often, such safety recommendations are divided into three sections: before, during, and after a hurricane strikes.

BEFORE THE HURRICANE

First, residents of hurricane-prone regions are advised to have a family disaster plan ready before the start of each hurricane season. This should include a checklist of things to do that includes the following:

- Gather enough food and water to last at least three days. A lot of the food should be canned in case the power goes out and cooking becomes impossible. As for water, the Red Cross advises having three gallons (11 liters) per person per day.
- Gather emergency items such as rain gear, a flashlight, a first-aid kit, and a battery-powered radio. During the emergency, someone should use the radio to get updates from a weather or news channel and/or an emergency broadcast channel.

- Board up windows to prevent or contain broken glass—particularly those residents who live along the coast.
- Pick up and store loose outdoor objects such as tools and trash barrels. Hurricane winds could potentially blow these items through house windows.
- Store valuables and important papers in watertight containers.
- Make sure to have some cash handy, because banks and cash-machines might close down during and/or just after the storm.
- Turn the refrigerator to its coldest setting. That way the inside will stay colder longer after the power goes out.
- Fill up the bathtub with water

A coastal resident boarded up the windows of his home in anticipation of an approaching hurricane.

make sure there is enough gas in the car. Also, plan for what to do with family pets. Many emergency shelters do not allow families to bring their pets. Next, determine the fastest and safest evacuation route. Finally, be sure that everyone in the family knows where to go. The American Red Cross advises:

Designate meeting places for your family if separated. In addition to your home, select a local church, school, or other pre-established location. Make sure each family member knows the address/contact informa-tion for your meeting places. Choose an out-of-state friend as a "check-in contact" for everyone to call. Make sure every member of your family knows the contact's phone number.

A New Orleans resident stocked up on water in preparation for 2008's Hurricane Gustav.

to use for cleaning during the emergency.

• Plan for possible evacuation. First,

Evacuation route signs are common in hurricane-prone areas such as St. Augustine, Florida.

during the storm. Mobile homes are far more likely to sustain damage than standard homes. Those who do stay home should remain inside during the hurricane. They should keep clear of unboarded windows, which might be shattered by flying debris.

Also, if local authorities order an evacuation during the storm, the family should comply. In that case, they should follow their prepared evacuation plan. They should avoid low-lying areas, where flooding is most likely.

Experts point out that some dangers still exist even after the hurricane is over. First, a parent or other adult should check for injured or trapped people. If someone is trapped in debris, someone should call 911 to request trained rescuers. Also, family members should not drink their tap

DURING AND AFTER THE HURRICANE

Most emergency authorities say people who live in mobile homes should go to designated local shelters

In August 2008, the southbound lane of I-10 West was closed to allow more traffic to travel north as New Orleans residents evacuated the city in the days before Hurricane Gustav's landfall.

water until local authorities say it is safe. Hurricanes often cause town water supplies to become polluted with sewage.

When venturing outside after the storm, stay away from standing pools of water, especially near power lines or poles. If the lines are down, the water could conduct a dangerous electrical current. And when driving, avoid floodwaters. These may hide deep holes or other road damage, which might cause the car to get stuck or sink. FEMA offers the following tips

*A pickup truck filled with floodwaters floated down a street in New Orleans'
Ninth Ward in the wake of Hurricane Rita; this storm reflooded an area
already devastated by Hurricane Katrina just weeks before.*

about dangers to look for and report:

Watch for washed out roads, contaminated buildings, contaminated water, gas leaks, broken glass, damaged electrical wiring, and slippery floors. Inform local authorities about health and safety issues, including chemical spills, downed power lines, washed out roads, smoldering insulation, and dead animals.

Hurricanes are huge and dangerous forces of nature. Whatever the cause, they are growing stronger. Meteorologists, hurricane hunters, and other weather scientists are working hard to understand them and make the public aware of extreme weather threats. Then everyone caught in their paths can have the best possible chance of surviving them.

1565
A hurricane scatters a French fleet, allowing the Spanish to capture a French fort in Florida

1780
The Great Hurricane of 1780 destroys numerous British ships docked in the Caribbean islands

1900
A large hurricane destroys most of Galveston, Texas, killing more than 8,000 people

1926–1960
The Atlantic Ocean produces more hurricanes each year than normal, possibly part of a natural cycle

1935
The so-called Labor Day Hurricane strikes the Florida Keys with winds of up to 200 mph (320 kph)

1944
The hurricane hunters, who fly into these storms to collect data, begin operations

1953
The U.S. National Hurricane Center begins giving hurricanes female names

1954
Hurricane Carol smashes into the east coast of the United States

1961
Typhoon Nancy hits Japan with 215-mph (344-kph) winds

1970
The Bhola Cyclone demolishes much of East Pakistan, killing more than 500,000 people

1971
Herbert Saffir and Bob Simpson devise the Saffir-Simpson scale to measure the comparative strength of hurricanes

1979
Experts begin alternating female hurricane names with male ones

2000
Hurricane Keith strikes southern Mexico, killing more than 40 people

2005
Hurricane Katrina strikes Louisiana and Mississippi, killing more than 1,800 people; Hurricane Rita strikes three weeks later

2007
Hurricane Dean, one of the few Category 5 hurricanes ever to make landfall, slams into eastern Mexico

2008
Hurricane Ike becomes the third most destructive hurricane in history, with nearly $32 billion in damages

Timeline

GLOSSARY

air pressure
force exerted by the weight of the molecules that make up air; usually, the lower the air pressure, the stronger the storm

Atlantic Multidecadel Oscillation
40- to 60-year cycle in which, many scientists think, hurricanes get stronger, then weaker, then stronger, and so forth

cyclone
name given to a hurricane that forms in the Indian Ocean or near Australia

dropsonde
device that scientists drop into hurricanes and tropical storms to measure and study them

eye
central, calm area at the center of a hurricane

eye wall
tall, vertical wall of fast-moving clouds lining the outer edge of a hurricane's eye

meteorologist
scientist who studies weather-related phenomena, including hurricanes

Saffir-Simpson scale
scale used by scientists to rate the comparative strength of hurricanes and their potential for damage

spiral bands
massive swaths of clouds that swirl around a hurricane's eye

storm surge
wall of water pushed forward by a hurricane's winds and low air pressure

tropical depression
ocean thunderstorm having winds of less than 39 mph (62 kph)

tropical storm
ocean thunderstorm having winds from 39 to 73 mph (62 to 117 kph)

typhoon
name given to a hurricane that forms in the western Pacific Ocean region

FURTHER RESOURCES

ON THE WEB

For more information on this topic, use FactHound.

1. Go to *www.facthound.com*
2. Choose your grade level.
3. Begin your search.

This book's ID number is 9780756540555

FactHound will find the best sites for you.

FURTHER READING

Fradin, Judy, and Dennis Fradin. *Witness to Disaster: Hurricanes.* Washington, D.C.: National Geographic, 2007.

Langley, Andrew. *Hurricanes, Tsunamis, and Other Natural Disasters.* Boston: Kingfisher, 2006.

Miller, Debra A. *Hurricane Katrina: Devastation on the Gulf Coast.* San Diego: Lucent, 2006.

Morris, Neil. *Inside Hurricanes and Tornadoes.* Milwaukee: Gareth Stevens, 2007.

Nardo, Don. *Global Warming.* Minneapolis: Compass Point Books, 2008.

LOOK FOR OTHER BOOKS IN THIS SERIES:

Climate Crisis: The Science of Global Warming

Collapse!: The Science of Structural Engineering Failures

Cure Quest: The Science of Stem Cell Research

Feel the G's: The Science of Gravity and G-Forces

Goodbye, Gasoline: The Science of Fuel Cells

Great Shakes: The Science of Earthquakes

Orbiting Eyes: The Science of Artificial Satellites

Out of Control: The Science of Wildfires

Rise of the Thinking Machines: The Science of Robots

SOURCE NOTES

Chapter 1: Damian Carrington. "Hurricane Katrina Devastates U.S. Gulf States." *New Scientist*. 30 Aug. 2005. 13 Oct. 2008. http://environment.newscientist.com/channel/earth/hurricane/dn7923-hurricane-katrina-devastates-us-gulf-states.html

Chapter 2: "Tropical Storm Dean Could Become Atlantic Hurricane." Reuters. 14 Aug. 2007. 13 Oct. 2008. www.reuters.com/article/domesticNews/idUSN14457520070814

Chapter 3: "How Strong Is That Hurricane? Just Listen." *Science Daily*. 10 April 2008. 13 Oct. 2008. www.sciencedaily.com/releases/2008/04/080410115330.htm

Chapter 4: Sarah Graham. "Hurricanes Getting Stronger, Study Suggests." *Scientific American*. 16 Sept. 2005. 13 Oct. 2008. www.sciam.com/article.cfm?articleID=00034565-DE1C-1329-9CE283414B7F0000

Chapter 5: Adam Nossiter. "New Orleans Sets Plan for Hurricane Evacuation." *The New York Times*. 29 Aug. 2008. 20 Oct. 2008. www.nytimes.com/2008/08/30/us/30gustav.html?partner=rssnyt

ABOUT THE AUTHOR

In addition to his numerous acclaimed volumes on ancient civilizations, historian Don Nardo has published several studies of modern scientific discoveries and phenomena. Nardo lives with his wife, Christine, in Massachusetts.

INDEX